World Stage Press

Verse from the Village

#InMySpaceOfHonesty
and Other Hashtags

October B.L.U.

World Stage Press
Verse from the Village

Praise for #InMySpaceOfHonesty and Other Hashtags

What a wild ride it has been digesting the word and the world of October B.L.U.!

IN MY SPACE OF HONESTY AND OTHER HASHTAGS has taken me into another world and down a rabbit hole that few have dared to reveal in such a stark light of experience.

"…peering through gun smoke and weed tokes [she] was born an urban baby…"
who has risen through the ranks of the forgotten and abused to peel the blinders off of eyes who refuse to vision her universe of what was and what now IS.

October B.L.U. pulls no punches and spares us no release from shared pain in her lifelong search for love and self acceptance.

From RACHET LOVE's memories of
"… cooked meals with 'reused grease
Understanding it adds flavor
Kind of love…"

To her emerging role as healer of herself and of others in LOVE NOTE #1

"Allow me to seamstress the frayed ends of your lifeless tapestry and collected pieces."

In her poem *APOLOGY* she writes
"...I'm sorry that I hide the fine print
and inactive ingredients from my mix..."

However I laud October B.L.U. for the courage that
it must have taken to reveal herself so thoroughly
to us.

I have learned something brilliantly constructive
from each of these soul filled poems and I expect
you will also!

Charlotte Hill O'Neal aka Mama C
Co founder United African Alliance Community
Center
Arusha, Tanzania

InMySpaceOfHonesty & Other Hashtags is an
example of unabashed storytelling. B.L.U.'s writing
drops readers into her experiences and allows
them to peer through her eyes from childhood to
acceptance. Fueled by vulnerability and raw word
play, we are privileged to see life, loss, love, and
the messiness of resurrection through her poetry
and her bravery.

With Gratitude,
Thea

World Stage Press
Verse from the Village

#InMySpaceOfHonesty and Other Hashtags
© 2018 Je'Ni Barrett
ISBN-13:978-0692195291
ISBN-10: 0692195297
Library of Congress Control Number: 2018958975

Printed in the United States of America

Layout Design by Emily Anne Evans

Cover Design by Emi Hasegawa

To my children, all of whom you can blame for any typos or poems you don't understand. They never respected the lights out momma off sign.

*To everyone still holding on to what doesn't serve you
.... let that shit go
Poison only kills the one who ingests it.*

To the last 4 minutes of my 5 minute morning meditation. We will meet soon my friend ... soon.

*To my best friend and biggest headache. We are in this for life!
Natural causes or....*

Well, you know. I'd be crazy to put it in writing. I've watched enough episodes of Snapped to have learned that lesson.

Nakupenda BTD

#dontjudgeme

#InMySpaceofHonesty

Table of Contents

#EASTIE

#WATERTHATCAUSESDEHYDRATION

#FOODTHATMALNOURISHES

❖ Short Story

EASTIE

noun

South Central Los Angeles, slang
An inhabitant of the Eastside of Los
Angeles

1. Having the resourcefulness needed
   to survive in an urban area

a) crafty

b) cunning

c) hustler

Cause

Birthed
brought home to the Nickerson Gardens
upgraded to the eastside
baptized and birth marked eastie
momma, daddy, auntie and uncles crack addicted
so I write

Molestations
abusive relationships
welfare recipient
my only inheritance
is why I write

Teenage mother
gave birth a month before I was 15
homeless
fragmented
fighting low self-esteem
all I could do was write

Growing pains
way past puberty
self-awareness
innerstanding
loving on me
grown woman hips and breast
#selfcare

Discovering sexy
way after sex
him
them
me

Dead black boys
water that causes dehydration
food that malnourishes
air that suffocates
bring back our girls

My little girls
for the little girl in me
my grown woman
finally nurturing

Thinking I wasn't enough
being too much
accepting
some fears
are best to let go

My God
Maat
oshun
amen
ogun
Amin
knowing that a prayer
needs no title
or agreed name
for this
I write

Who left the door open?

Real talk, I hate flies
thought they only lived a day
them buzzing bastards

Wire Frames

I'm starting to think it's the glasses
maybe
the way I can't help but smile
even when uncomfortable

Unwanted approaches
aggressive intentions
are finding their way into my space
a little too often these days

Raised with good manners
just a few years into embracing my womanhood
let's be clear
I keep hair ties and tennis shoes nearby
because I still fight

Nicknamed Ever-ready
I was raised on the eastside
aka Ruff-House
proper spoken and educated
#blacknerdsrock

Let these words sound off warning signs
life lessons can find themselves
on the other side of ass whoopings
and black eyes
nicknamed Ever-Ready

Second to the youngest of 12 girls
you always had to leave some
to take some
I handle mines
aka Ruff-House

Feeling froggy
leap
I'm quiet for a reason
prey
never hears the hunter's gun cock
during hunting season

Between Hooper and Naomi

I grew up believing the stars shined brighter
in my eastside reality
then they did
in others west side dreams

Vision kind of hazy
peering through gun smoke
and weed chokes
I was born an urban baby

Similac first meals
seeming to lack for nothing
yet everything
at the same time
my block seemed long
during my short-legged days

Had no shame busting out my 5-dollar book of food
stamps
when the donut truck hit the block
back doors open
drawers pulled out
1 glaze twist, 1 old fashion
a few extra donut holes
I bought as payment
to get the best girls to turn at Double-Dutch

Before the street lights came on
hit the corner store for a RC cola
a pack of now&laters
watermelon flavored
and a note from my auntie

*"This is Miss Jackie, send me a soft pack of
Benson and Hedges menthol with my niece."*

Still had enough change for a giant icee
cherry flavored
blackberry clearly canadian
and a pack of salty plums
with 5 dollars
I reigned on my block

Friday nights
head to the high school
navigating past the
dog guarded
unlocked gates
eastside safari
making it just in time
to be hit by the sweet funky scent of elotes
one dollar gets you the works
parmesan, paprika, butter, lime, and mayonnaise
we never questioned the mayonnaise

Saturday morning
the loud but distant sound
a squeeze horn and off-key soprano
TAMALES!!!!!!!
my alarm clock
rushed out the door sliding in house shoes
I didn't wear slippers until my adult years
one effortless motion
dressed and out the door
snatching up last 2 queso tamales

out of the black trash bag lined pots
no champurrado
I preferred carnations instant coco
somehow
always forgot the salsa

Rushing to get back to the house
cheap meals and morning smokes
brought the cute boys out
messy head
forgotten scarf
I didn't want the neighbors to clown

I grew up seeing the stars shine brighter
in my eastside reality
cause they did
it was family
revolt
backyard gardens
unrest
bloods and crips
2.25 miles in total
I cherished my little piece of it
between Hooper and Naomi

I am

Baby's breath tucked neatly
in freshly pressed ponytails
worn for Easter morning service
ruffled white panties
matching socks
underneath my favorite pink dress

Breath
smelling like
orange juice and glazed doughnut
a treat for those who got up early enough
to make it to Sunday school

I am
youth choir membership vet
trying to work my way up to the usher-board
there was something about being in control of
handing out the church fans
and tithing envelopes

Depending on how friendly you were
you could get the new
crisp
unused fans
the ones with the local funeral homes
advertising its family special

Or
The limp
bent in half
no matter how hard you wave it
you ain't getting any cooler fan
something about being the first at the door
when all the other members walk in

The rush of energy you get
from having a front row seat
clear view of all the commotion
deacons
jumping out their seats
in an almost choreographed
fall to the floor

Numbness in my right hand
from holding it behind my back
feet hurt from standing
1 hour past the time church was supposed to end
but the whole church is
still in praise and worship
I couldn't dream of a better place to be

Handing out
my third box of tissues
I was like a psychic
when it came to who would break down next
passing the box through the pews
faster than the collection plate
which
always rushed down
after a good testimony
tears easily make purses and wallets appear

In the middle of pastors call and repeat
request for the building fund
and love offerings would sneak in
them his and hers Cadillacs
ain't gon' gas themselves

I am
in church from morning to evening break
replacing song books

in the neatly hidden pocket
behind each pew
now that no one's watching
I stand in front of the pulpit
looking at the empty sanctuary
pretending
to be GOD

In these moments of silence
I feel it
that connection
that transcends time
judgment
experience
and hurt

I am
prayer
making its way from soul
into thoughts
into words
too afraid to be spoken
it seems all others
have gone unanswered

Too afraid to complain
raised to believe
in the strength of mustard seeds
blind steps
extraordinary shoulder strength
I'm left feeling
spiritually inadequate

I become doubt
fixed in a space of worry
wrapped neatly in confusion
full of fear

I am every sin
trying so desperately to win favor
scared to waste an eternity
waiting on the return of a savior
I
am
the answer
already

Cast blasphemous
just thinking about
speaking about
being whole in my broken

I become church
silently collecting my pieces
holding them so tight
religion can't see the cracks in them
uncomfortably
making everyone else feel better

While they reach out
we all hold hands
bow our heads
now we prey

24 Hours

I was tricked
one week out
from the start of the summer
my immune system
was sleeping on the job

I felt it coming on
tried to head it off
boost of vitamin c
echinacea tea
having a cold in 104-degree heat
was not
what I planned for

Foot-in pajamas
extra socks on
slices of onion on the bottom of my feet
google it, it's a thing
#homeremedies

I counted down and added up
8 solid hours of sleep
tomorrow
I'll be putting garlic in everything I drink
positive thoughts
what you think will be
Snuggled in
vicks vaporub on chest
couldn't reach my back
no help from family because
they say I got cooties
24-hour bug
I wasn't worried

4 hours later
With tissue stuck to the tips of my fingers
and stuffed in my right nostril
can't breathe out the left
I'm suffocating
trying to clear my throat of this thick
post nasal drip
feeling more like cooling lava

3 hours of damn infomercials
no energy to find the remote
all I want
is to swallow
without bracing myself for impact
and gripping the sheets
my mom said
all I had to do was
eat some vicks
never mind them warning labels
folks been doing this for years

Don't judge me
for some relief
I was ready to accept
turpentine oil poisoning

Hot salted water
gargle
tears
spit…
repeat

Alcohol in the freezer
I have to break this fever
second hot totty
trying to get some sleep

drool on the pillows
up the side of my face
and in my hair

Under blankets
freezing
and sweating
at the same time
soaking my sheets

Hot flash
covers on the floor
I swear these 24 hours
feels like eternity

Squatter

I never thought of my childhood as different or weird. I would have never considered us homeless or squatters - a term I didn't learn until my twenties. When momma introduced me to Sonny (they called him Sy or Scientist), I thought he was nice. He had nice eyes. But, his nose was a different story. It reminded me of Skeletor, the bad guy from the He-Man cartoon. It was difficult to make eye contact at first. I didn't want to seem rude, if caught staring at his "nose area." Momma spent all day telling me how I would have my own room, my own bed, toys and all! It was a far better set up than what I had at my grandmother's house. There were 9 of us in a one-bedroom apartment. Until 6 months ago, I lived with my grandparents (Doc and Annie May), my father James, older sister Fanita, little cousin Anniemarie (she liked being called Ann Marie) and her mom, my aunt (Niece). I know the math isn't adding up. The 3-extra people, I'm not sure who they were. One day after my daddy and granny had been gone for a few days, they came in, woke up the whole house, banging on the front door. Someone lost the key. My dad was still wearing my Halloween costume. He put it on when he couldn't find a shirt 3 months ago. My grandmother seems to have lost her bottom dentures… again; now arguing with one of the strangers about where she'd last had them. One hand on her hip, the other against the wall for balance.

"Bitch", my grandmother said, "I handed them to you when you got up to go to the kitchen at John Roberts' house."

"Ain't no way", the other lady responded, "why would I ever touch some nasty ass teeth! You know I don't mess around."

My grandmother yelled back, "If I'm lying, I'm flying and we both standing flat on da flo'. Yo' drunk ass just don't remember shit. You always act up when you get a lil' drank in yo' system." to which the lady responded in a poem of sorts.

"Gin make you sin. That brown liquor, you'll give it up quicker. Cisco or Old E. It makes no difference to me. French, Spanish, or English. Say it wit me. A drunk ain't shit."

"Ann, Homier already told you he gotem," said the other stranger with the air tank on wheels. Although strong and direct in his opinion, you couldn't really hear what he said. He wore a white band around his neck that connected to a small white box. Every time he spoke, he would put a piece of tissue over the box. Breathy, raspy sentences would follow along with a mucus filled cough. I'm not sure what forced me awake more violently, the turning on of every light, screaming matches, snot coughs, or their body odor - a witch's brew of musty armpits, mildewed shoes, alcohol and morning-overdue-for-a-toothbrush breath, added to the unmistakable chemtrail of sherm. This, was the come down, after days of crack binging.

"Honey, are you ready?"
"Yes momma."

"Do you remember what we talked about?"

"Yes momma."

"We gotta check you in school, after we get your bags in the house. Remember I told you, you don't tell them people nothing about your grandmother's house. All they need to know is you live with me. We just moved over here, near the new school."

"Yes momma. I remember like last time. I always remember because I'm smart."

"Yes, you are."

Momma gave me the biggest smile. We walked up to a locked gate and 3 barking dogs ran to the gate jumping over each other. I was so scared; I almost ran in the streets. My mom grabbed my arm and told me, these were the dogs we talked about. I imagined small cute puppies. Two of the dogs were bigger than me!

Sonny came out and told the dogs to "chill out" and they did. I thought well if it's that easy, I'll be ok. Sonny invited us in and although there was no front door, or windows. As soon as I walked in, it felt like a home. We walked into what was supposed to be the living room. Off to the right was an empty kitchen. We didn't have standard kitchen stuff like, a sink, stove, or fridge, but Sonny set up a nigga-rigged stovetop on the back porch. The bottom was a metal trash can he filled with wood and coals, topped off with a metal piece from a grocery store cart. He used this as a stove top. Two pots were boiling, one with water. The other had what would become one of my favorite meals: SpaghettiOs, Denti-Moore beef stew and rice all mixed together. After dinner, Sonny did the best he could to make me feel comfortable. He formally introduced me to the dogs, Chino, Lady and Sweetie, and they seemed to like me. Sweetie was the puppy. I was told the other puppies died. Which made Lady very protective of her only surviving puppy. I was warned not to pick her up right away. It was getting dark and Sonny started lighting candles. Candles lined every window seal and counter in the house. It was the most beautiful thing I had ever seen. It felt like a fairytale. The flickering candle lights danced, and I created shadow puppets for hours. The soft glow seemed to lessen the reality that we didn't have electricity, gas or running water.

Baths were taken in extra-large paint buckets. On the better days when it wasn't cold outside, the stove topped boiled water stayed hot longer. On the worst days, there was no coal for hot water. Cold water with a little rubbing alcohol for added cleanliness had to do. The second bucket, pushed to the furthest part of the bathroom, was for number 1 and number two. I was happy to be at school and walking distance to KFC during the day for normal bathroom breaks. No matter what, home was home. And for the first time, in a long time, it felt like family. Sweetie got on my nerves, much like a younger sibling. We'd fight all the time. She would always steal my stuff. She chewed up all my shoes, including the new pair of hand-knitted house shoes I got from a neighbor. Chino, was like a protective big brother. He'd walk me to school every day, but Mondays were the most adventurous. We'd have to run through the alley to get away from the dog catchers. Over the next few years, Sonny would provide the best example of a father. Our squatters space, would be the fondest memory of a home.

Strangers

I sat with strangers
as they removed your
cold
stiff
body from the house

Big sister mad at me
asking why you got no tears from me
not knowing
he spent years
fostering fears in me
that would last
until last days
and amongst peers for me

I can remember
a sense of relief
synapse sending signals to nerve endings
trying to reach my inner innocence
to let her know
it was done

My uniformed
wasn't an open invitation
my adolescence
wasn't a beckoning
for your so-called
admiration

I sat with strangers
as they removed your
lies
secrets

and insecurities
from that house

All while
re-playing me
laying eyes wide open
hoping
that someone
would just so happen
to stop by

Replaying me
laying there
hoping
Pat Seajack
would somehow
give Vanna the cues
to reveal the words
H E L P   H E R

I sat with strangers
as they removed
your body wrapped in
my self-worth
from that house

Now just because of you
I sat alone
no tears
empty
with more than enough fears
surrounded

by all these strangers

Bubble

*Sing - My bubble, my bubble,
where ever I go, you go,
my bubble, my bubble,
my bubble and me!

Had a
near miss of meeting someone new today
as they approached
I pretended there was something on my android
that needed my attention more
and couldn't wait

Offered my
business card
no direct connects
just my Facebook
Twitter
and Instagram handles
all fake personas of who I think I am
hoping
they don't want to get know who I am
that's
when judgement happens

We
like
but rarely comment
thinking it's big to pay homage
with a retweet of other's comments
we may never meet

Feeling
connected

if a chance friending
resulted in an inbox
and be the first
to repost an e-vite
to an invite
with no intentions of attending

Attending would prove
we just spent all of this time pretended
and well…
these bubbles
can't handle that kind of offended

I claim
I don't shake hands
because
I don't know where yours have been
truth is
I'd have to let go of my personal comfort zone
fight against gravity
enter into a physical agreement
that states
you're allowed
in
my bubble
Now
I can't keep up with the number of
times we've made contact
and the amount of Purell
I have left
inside my purse

I saw it on the news today
a new strain of
A-Hep-Fluenza was discovered
they've uncovered

its origins
are from everywhere
the only safe place
is inside my bubble

In this bubble
I don't have to worry about
anyone getting too close
when they decide to leave
causing me hurt

Its confirmed on all my social media feeds
these feelings of needed isolation
are warranted
bubbles can be known by
many names
anthropophobia,
agoraphobia,
awkward,
loner
ADHD
or just different

But if you're feeling fancy
social anxiety disorder
they all come with meds
although
not clinically diagnosed
when I googled
all my symptoms matched
on web MD

Now that I fit the criteria
all my new
unwarranted
untested

meds
are free!
that's fine by me
after all the irreversible side effects
my bubble,
is the only place I'd want to be

These bubbles, are starting to define us
where we don't go
what we don't eat
why we don't speak
I know, it's not just me
Maybe movies like
13 reasons
and Dear White People
aren't so much about tensions
but the subconscious
intention
of suspensions
of getting to know another person

It's only going to get worse
we'll never
get to know each other
through Snapchat
Facebook
Instagram
or hypo-allergenic gloves

Roots Track Old-school A and B Side

Track A

My grandmother
died on our bathroom floor
smoking crack
it wasn't her first time
just
her last
that day
gathered 'round gurney
paramedics completed mandatory S.O.P.s
defibrillation tabs
connected to lines of hopelessness
stuck to the top of her left
and missing right breast

Five inches of keloid scars
looking more like
overused railroad tracks
was all that cancer left
concaved frame
covered a heart
that would no longer beat

Living with diabetes for 10 years
requiring insulin injections
the last 4 of those
ate books of matches
and crushed ice
to replenish lacking minerals
my grandmother
was far from feeble

Kept her crack pipe
neatly tucked in the wads of toilet tissue
she used to stuff her bra
always said
"nobody got to know what ain't or is under my
clothes"

After some trial and error
we all learned
just how many rotations around hand
she needed
to fill out her aged
loose skinned
b cup bra with
she
wasn't a fan of wearing panties

Barely 5 feet
soft caramel candy skin tone
coffee stained
never glued in dentures
a smile
that started in her eyes
matriarch of lost tribe

Co-dependency
predispositions
and the love for creamy grits
salt, sugar, canned milk, black pepper and extra
butter
knowing the perfect ratio of her iced coffee
to brown liquor
is all she had left in her to pass down
this
far more than what she inherited

Born to teenage mother
father
we don't talk about that

Unhealthy relationships
connected her to cracked realities
long before cocaine got introduced

She
gave birth to potted palm trees
whose seedlings never knew
their confinement lead to rotted roots
wore the stink of Easter's forgotten eggs
like expensive perfume
allowed us girls to toast the New Year
with alcohol infused eggnog
we felt connected

Track B
I won't pretend to understand the secret
a pound of chicken
bought from Parks meat market
which always smelled like
athlete's foot
and morning breath
awaited the blessings of grandma's hot lard
in cast iron skillet
baptism

Brown paper bag
rolled tight under clinched fist
she'd shake
squinted eyes
looking over her glasses
shake

puffs of flour pushed through bottom left and right
sides
of the weathered brown bag
not sure what clouded the room more
flour
or the puffs of smoke
snaking its way from her cigarette

Slipknot halo
dangling from the left side of her mouth
ashes hanging on like
a child with separation anxiety
she'd point
"Grab a pinch of flour and toss it in the skillet"
"Test if it's ready"
homemade brown gravy
bits of burned chicken skin
fried flour
milk and onions
poured over fluffy
perfectly cooked
long grain white rice
"You got to clean the starch off
"Don't measure"
"Eyeball it"
middle finger in the pot
first joint rice
second joint water
add salt

"Good seasoning ain't never kill nobody"
"Only thang promised"
"We all leaving here anyway"

I'll always wonder
if she had any regrets

Kinsfolk

Understanding written recipes
are only suggestions
grandma's biscuits
were always made with extra butter
it's how they browned
melanin
imbedded in perfection
like

Summertime at yo play-cousins house
not blood-related
somehow spirit
connects linage
like red wood roots
sturdy
we be family

Through fall outs
funerals
new births
or
corners of juice
left in the jug
hidden in the back of the fridge
like you just couldn't drink
that last lil bit you left

It's the looks of concern
and condolence
After the whopping you got
because mama found out you did it
empathy

We
feel we
sun up
Frankie Beverly and Gap band
add background
cards or dominoes out
kickbacks are never planned
just a Friday
somebody told somebody
on the day
somebody got paid

Drinks and grill going
we share wash rags
and swigs from the water-hose close
safe shelter for block stretches
our neighbors
made up our hoods
familial protection

Black trash bags
industrial size
turn dry grass patches
into water-slides
don't worry about the rub burns
on your hips and thighs
aloe vera
grows in everybody's backyard
somewhere near the collard greens

My people
we make monuments from ant hills
the blueprints of pyramids
prototype for Lawry's seasoning
is in our DNA

Genius
tasted in aunty mac and cheese
her foot in it
was an accepted ingredient
who's bringing the potato salad
was the defining question
at any impromptu celebration

Lasting memories
found between
new and old school music
sis
showing Lil James
that the hustle and electric slide
are one in the same
we all step on the 2 and 4

Instinctively
heartbeats
syncopate
to base line drum beats
we literally feel the music
we are the music
you feel me

WATERTHATCAUSESDEHYDRATION

verb/adjective

*Can only be combated by self-care

1. The active pursuit of something/
   someone you think you need but
   don't.

a) codependency

b) lust

c) toxic connections

Love Note # 1

Allow me to seamstress the frayed ends of your
lifeless tapestry and collected pieces

Argu-texting

You mean to tell me
after hours of text messages
containing cleverly strung together quotes
no curse words
great examples of comparison
I still don't get a fucking apology

Concisely pointed out errors
demonstrating
how you
and only you
caused this conflict
this confusion
this break in communication
you still don't give a damn enough
to just say it....

I keep checking my phone
logging in and out of
social media accounts
checking my ringer volume
even though it's on loud
reading
and re-reading the text feeds
somehow hoping I missed it

Where is all that love
love you laid at my feet
this argument
will be different
my tone

even though we're argu-texting
so 2016
my tone
is different
I used all your favorite emoji's
at any moment
you'll recognize
I'm not even using CAPS
it was all you
this time

You see them hearts in every other line
I know you'll apologize
I am your everything
#relationshipgoals

We
spent days plotting against the world
you remember
Bonnie and Clyde thangs
You promised me you were
different

Voicing my opinion
seems to have been lost in text-lation
this
should have been
a face to face conversation

What part of the game is this
what about the promises
all you had to do was say you were sorry

I admit
sending just the letter K
I knew you knew what I really meant
#childish
my innocence didn't live here

Insults turn energy in to assholes
this makes no sense
lines drawn
placed behind unread messages
wish you spent more time listening

Senseless jabs
in angry truths
cut deep
if only yesterday's love space
allowed you to hear me
today
I should've just picked up the phone
asked you to talk face to face

Sisterhood

Words are like deaf pit bulls
once you let them go
you can't call them back

She wonders why her demise
seems to be the theme
of your every conversation

Committed to your words
like
amphetamines to meth
causing catastrophes
with every breath
you speak words of
discouragement

Sling blades of
mental malnourishment
ending your forked-tongue lullabies
with disconnected
I love you's
baby
I want you's

Why can't you just
fall back
to get ahead
or just give some
this
is the only way
she thinks he will listen
to her pleas of
no one will ever love you
like this one

Or

I just want to be his only this one

Not considering
he just uses them
to wipe off the bottom of his shoes
when he's finished
walking all over
that one

When will you realize
you are more than
that one
find the strength in your spine
your DNA sacrificed splitting atoms to create

You were born with the ability
to learn from your crawl
how to walk
you were blessed
with the innate understanding of the need
to flee or fight
I choose the latter

Even if
just on your behalf
I beg you not to listen to the chatter
of other lost souls
who encourage you to
love him
past his flaws
STD's aren't flower arranged gifts
sis
you
deserve better
than this

If I have to stand on your mountain top
neglect my own
scream from it
in hopes that the echoes you hear
make it back through
I love you

It may not be the love you're looking for
at least
you won't have to look no more
I can embrace you with the love of a mother
sister
and a friend
all at the same time
with 3 times the LOVE
you will always win

With the well-thought-out blueprint
of the human anatomy
my one month
and two ears
means
I have more time to listen to your fears
two hands to work overtime
whipping away your tears
more strength in my lower
than my upper
to hold you steady
when you can't do so on your own

I offer more than just
late nights alone

I can offer a sisterhood
that will allow you to grow strong in your storm
let those infested

no-good man branches fall off
so that your spirit can grow
realizing again
you are a beautiful person
and deserve to be treated as so

We won't go around singing songs of unwanted
scrubs
sending out bill pay requests
or allow you to find comfort in being
someone's weekend lover

But
we'll pray for your patience
as your King
protector
provider
finds his way to your left seat

I'll never guesstimate how long that will be
I offer words of encouragement
until you both meet

My Side

Picture perfect painted on stage
your representative was amazing
grown man shoes
never wanted a prince
would've bet it all
I found my King in you

Your charming is what disarmed me
life lived through monologues
you loved to hear yourself talk
I shouldn't have been surprised
you missed all the queues
when I said listen
we need to talk

Finding myself doing all the talking
created emotional cages
you perfected
used car salesman tactics
I made the mistake of telling you what I wanted
trusted my broken pieces in your hands
craftsmanship crafty
so skilled
passed off toothpaste for Elmer's glue
paper mache dreams of forever
only to pop hope's balloon

It was all so childish
pain so heavy
I was forced to lose a few
my health was being affected
had no choice but to drop you

Please note
fishing in swimming pools
speaks nothing to your abilities
I was prey ready for the taking
you saw my injuries
momentary weakness
preparation laced
falsely boasted king's lineage
tried to ruin my Queendom

Bloodline of warriors
you weren't even kin to them
I believed in you
bought into your visions of you
even though no proof ever seen
your words
my bond into make believe truths
it was never about the connections

Lost in the presentations
honesty left diseased and uncared for
barely noticeable
disregarded
scraps of reality
you left on the cutting room floors
of all your past
present
and future relationship tragedies

But I don't blame you
every disrespectful word
that came out of your mouth
was a blessing to me

I know you don't innerstand now
over exposure to feces

helps to build up immunities
the next time
I find myself amidst actions of inconsistency
I'll have enough strength to recognize
strategize quick exit scenes

Maturity
I don't blame all of you
dances
resulting in one with bruised toes
takes two left feet
I'm thankful
healing
is in the acceptance of
personal responsibilities

I know I'll heal
with scars
I'll never be ashamed of
I'll heal

Allowing the traces of dried tears to linger
letting others see
I survived the spaces between heartbreak
and simple beats
reminding me
I can still hear the music

I created the fucking melodies

Apology

After what seemed like
100 ways to start this
starting off with
it wasn't you
it was me
is just way too cliché

I want it to come off more poetic
something like
the moons and the stars
didn't have a chance to
align with the oceans and seas
in the true moments
we were meant to be

But
I'm afraid I might lose you
the last thing I want
is for my long drown out
over-thought apology
to be wasted in spaces
of further misunderstanding
So
I'll stand here

Big girl priorities in place
simply say
I
am
sorry

I'm sorry that I hide the fine print
and inactive ingredients

from my mix
I'm sorry that
I saw you coming from a mile away
which gave me time to recruit my best
representative
and present her
your way

It's almost sad to say
you never saw it coming
a past rooted in abuse
misuse
and a personal vow of
I bet I'll leave you first
rather than be the first to get hurt
while you were planting lilies for the springtime
I was hiding landmines
in fields of nonexistent excuses
because even though not spoken
I heard them all

No amount of loving me
could crumble walls
built by adolescent
coping mechanisms
reinforced by past hurts

Never forgotten birthdays
or anniversaries of first dates
couldn't heal the belief
that my value
would ever reach past
the length of my skirt

See
this little girl
fronting behind
a well-dressed woman's mask
was simply not ready
not ready to admit
I never had love
therefore
unequipped to be love
or recognize love
when you appeared

Instead
I just peered through murky idealisms
of what this was supposed to be
judging you
on all that had come before you
not being willing to admit
their faults
were direct reflections of me
In time
I hoped my well-fitted facade
would start to feel like second skin
but all those eternally stuffed lies
began to take up all my time
I was finding myself preoccupied
trying to conceal
the festering wounds
I pretended had healed

When I finally had to admit

Molded bread
wasn't the same as penicillin
sexual healing
only made sense as song lyrics

because sheets
were no place
for mentally stunted little girls
never taught
she could hold on to her pearls
thought them cast amongst swine
was worthy of her time
because they gave her props
on trending timelines

I'm sorry that
in times of disagreement
you were hurt by the fine lines
my words spilled over
from voicing my opinion
to outright disrespect
and hell
if I never get another chance
to say how I feel
or what I really meant
I'm sorry
it wasn't the real me
that you met

Our Daily Bread

Over exposure of nudity
singular vision
I'd rather get naked

Take day trips
exploring with hands
features
and emotions
eye contact
no prescriptions

Allowing
soul connections
to take effect
get to know me
knowing
is to get all of me

Offer you
to ingest me
daily

Bare battle wounds
healing
scars and all
we
kamikaze
every negative spoken on this binding

They will never know the offering
who are they
to God our sins anyway

Unknown sacrifice
They don't know this work

We continue to pull back these layers
embrace uncomfortable
in the familiar
show me your insecurities
I'll praise in tongues
they're my favorite part
of your imperfect

allow me reverence

acknowledged my praise

reciprocate

Ratchet Love

I want that Lucious and Cookie kinda love,
that kinda unconditional loyalty
a homeless man
has for his dog
kinda love

You gotta admit
there's nothing like
that kinda love

The kind of love that will
have you both at the county building
starting your own cases
so there will be double the food stamps
kind of love

The kind of love that will have you handing me the
phone
telling creditors
you're not home
while they're trying to collect on the jewelry bill
for the ring
I got on

We in the same home
but you're not on the lease
to avoid section 8 increases
I want the kind of unexplainable
hood raised attainable
undeniably
what some may call
ratchet
kinda Love

I'll know
when we don't have chips
cards are missing from the deck
walls have started to crumble
from the pressure of rocks and hard places
we got each other's back
the kind of love that doesn't mind
signing the W.I.C. checks
you know a full breakfast comes next
there's no problem eating off the two for one
or splitting a five-dollar foot long

The kind of love
that can be found
in a bowl
of top ramen noodles
yours with hot sauce
mine
with a slice of cheese
but
I need a bite of yours
to make mines taste better
and you don't mind
kinda love

Looking forward to birthdays
we get to dine at benihana for free
catching the bus
using yo mama's access card
to get us to the museum
no entrance fee
thanks to EBT

proudly posting
we're going on a date
kinda love

The kind of love that
can find romance in sleeping in the car
extra blankets
shared pillow
because our living situations ain't so great

No judgment
unconditional
will stand against him
her
them
and my past
just to show how much love we have
cooked meals with reused grease
understanding it adds flavor
kind of love

I want the kind of love where
we share our dreams
even though nowhere near complete
we wear each other's success on our sleeves
misunderstood from outsiders looking in
deemed
lost cause
side eyes of
they could do better
but we know better

This love
stripped of everything
but love
will most certainly
last forever

#WCMCeveryday

Status update
…is in a relationship

Daily hashtags of anniversary dates
that haven't reached their anniversary
us-ies
in heavy rotation
picture tags
shout outs
just in case the other stuff was missed
full conversations under posts
even though we're sitting
right next to each other
slick one liners
just for the insiders
liking
and sharing
required
phones on vibrate
cause conflict
breakups
confirmed through passive aggressive memes
…feeling like song titles
#feelingaggy
deleting the new cheating
blocking worse than divorce
privacy settings on custom
just enough to keep up
friend request
sent to a friend
of friends
friend

hoping
you'll come across a new pic
picking out everything wrong
with the new chick's outfit
#basicbitch
best freakum dress on
flash
click
filters popping
new background flick
new profile pic
cause you know
he'll see it

Good Moaning

Woke up thinking about your lips
feeling their imprint
left cheek pressed to my pillow
I hear my heart beats clearly
increasing tempo
with every leg movement
slow
deliberate grinds against my palms
thoughts of intimate embraces
awake
eyes closed
to keep the fantasy visual

I can smell you
striped of cologne
its natural
I can taste your wants
in every
remembered kiss
lubrication
signals reciprocation
you
are
received
if only you were here

Finger tips signal desires
in the hours before dawn breaks
it's the best illumination
no filters needed
cerebral sensations
I can't wait to see you

counting down hours
distance play aphrodisiac
to yoni symphonies
and all I want to do is
sing

The Pit

I feel safest in the crease of his left arm pit
nestled below his chin
warmth of his chest
my left shoulder near his ribs
it's where I rest

This prolonged pose
causes his shoulder to ache
he lets me believe
my comfort
eases his pain

Heavy breathing
serenades me cradlesong sleep
hearts beat deep beneath tired bones
and heavy bodies
I place my right hand over his brave
I pray for him
most of the time
silent
most of the time
tears
most of the time
fearing I didn't praise him enough in our wake
to meet with God
on his behalf
I always ask for forgiveness

Find myself lost in chatter type conversations
about how I would have never guessed
his broken
and my broken

made healed
not perfect
kintsugi*
imperfections dusted in gold
celebrating we did the work
found worthy
blessed into enough
no explanations needed

This love
is
nothing less than
the hardest work on monument
bare hands
pre-technology
we be pyramids
committed
standing tested
through funding loss
unforeseen
on purpose
personally caused
setbacks
it's in this space
I rest

On nights where sleep
slips into next day hours
I snuggle in and wait
inhale every scent of masculine
exhaling new found feminine
balanced and anchored
I rest

*kintsugi: a Japanese art of repairing broken pottery with
 lacquer dusted or mixed with powdered gold, silver, or
 platinum.

Cosmic Love

We
pinky swear love promises
because only our touch
is needed to fulfill them

Just for fun
we wet lips full of passion
kiss to seal them
hands in places
too private to share them
we be to love
what water be to this planet

He plants kisses so deeply
I can only remember them in afterthoughts
after title waves of energy
our synergy is awakened
we've known each other long before time
our together life purposes
were conducted
and constructed
in the stars
if you look at just the right angles
on the clearest of nights
our mapped-out destiny still stands

Easy as any of them dippers to finger trace
for hopefuls still waiting
on their love spaces
to be revealed
his kind of love
it healed

His kind of love
birthed me new realities
where in others
I wasted time just existing
persisting that
good enough
was just that
when all we had to do
was just be
allow the universe
to remind us of we

we had time
none of our life lessons were for free
we paid our dues in lost time
incurred fines
trying to read between the lines
trying to reprogram
what was predestined
because life
wasn't fitting within our perceived time lines

But we found us
now he
is forever mine
this is the
we will be together
even in the next life time kind
besides our children
we are each other's everything
he is all I'll ever need
sexy
educated
and sensitive
with a sense of humor

that may be caught on a 24-hour delay
But

We laugh deep belly laughs
and we like it that way
his demeanor
has most fooled
into thinking he's a teddy bear
believe me when I say
he is a grizzly
step anywhere into the space of disrespect
you're guaranteed to inherit problems so complex
it would take generations
to solve them

Imhotep insight
he is my friend
my protector
my King

Him

Simply being him
allows me
to be a better me

Cleanse

Emotional space
Mother nature's due process
Eve blessing and cure

IKEA You

First impressions
baked cinnamon rolls
mixed with the scent of
Swedish meatballs
weird
but somehow goes together

You accept it
open
bright
everyone enjoying structured space
instructions
even a map with directions
making it clear where this is going
you
are where you're supposed to be
every now and then
you may get a little lost
but no fear or worry
you've just discovered something
you never knew
you were looking for

Everything easy
everything has a place
it all makes sense on the show room floor
the extra pillows make for decoration
inside of cluttered spaces
options open
yet limited to your budget
measured moments
for good measure

color choices and compromises made
it won't be long
until you call this newness home

Check outs
long and slow
made easy with close
feel good treats
it feels like solidarity
it feels like common interest
it feels like you get in
to get out
to get in line again
but the drama
is worth it
you can see a payoff
everyone else
is doing the same work
compare savings and DIY projects
there's hope and excitement
until you get home

Behind closed doors
they looked better
under bright lights
the easy assemble
quick put together
it should fit
presented well with my ideas of new pieces
in my old spaces
things aren't lining up
my lefts
aren't fitting just right
missing screws and bolts
can't even understand the instructions

now questioning the max weight
and missing slats
plywood boards
flimsily straps
supposed to hold all of us together
what you saw in the store
can't be the same
as what you brought home

Misled
investments made in fraudulent wood stains
the headboard doesn't even match the frame
outraged
hours spent looking for that mystery tool
you want to give up
until you're reminded
the work
was always a part of the bargain

Damn Kids

Today is a day of liberation
in this moment
I'll raise my hands
inhale enough
to loudly exhale
I DON'T LIKE MY DAMN KIDS
sometimes

I know I'm not alone but
I won't press you to enjoy this free
I be Harriet Tubman in this
so
if you decide to stay
just don't get in the way
of my forward movement

What's in this for me
they don't appreciate me
hours spent
folding towels
bed bath and beyond style
#mommagotskills

Finding and matching socks
so they have
matching socks
baking soda
vinegar
lavender scented bleach in the wash
just so they can decide
it's easier to sleep on the mattress
with no sheets

In the kitchen cabinets
every label facing forward
canned goods
lined up by size
for easy access to ravioli

Even though I was told
this processed
heavy-salted
gag for red sauce
was better
than what I had homemade
I still serve it
with a side salad
and a smile
now guess who decides
they're allergic to kale

No one ever notices
the closet organization
the shirts and jackets
hung neatly
facing the same way
because they all end up in a pile
on the floor
then back in the dirty clothes bags
I promise
I just don't like them
sometimes

I know
every bit of this is taboo

mommy just supposed to do
but
I was here first
seniority counts in any other situation
if I could
I'd drop them off
at the nearest safe baby location
but I called
they said something about
age limits
the oldest
is only 180 months

Where else can you willingly
not follow every direction you're given
eat all the food
including all the snacks for you
and the
ONE
I bought for me
where can you stay
rent free
use every light
rolls of tissue
NOT
put back on the holder
and still have demands
about what you want to eat

I come home after 9 hours of working
cook
well-balanced
grains
vegetables
protein

and you have the nerve to
request noodles

I can't make this up
the middle one
shaved his newly sprouted face fuzz
in my kitchen
said
he didn't want to wait
to get in the bathroom

I'm done
today
I declare my independence
I will not be treated like
the brown part of the banana

ANYMORE!

Baby Hair

The test
brown paper bag
pencil falling or not
from tangled
or straight hair

Foundation skin tone matches
indoctrinated with should be's
in beauty standards
from centuries ago
2010 skin color ranking
produce
the same melanin negative results

Allowing my beautiful copper brown girls
to be infected with Disney's subliminal
watching Brave
they found comfort
sleeping on their beauty
Finger tips
in coiled q's
She said
she really wants pretty hair

Cozy carpet turned
egg shell delicate
in my reply
confirmation
admiration
of her strong follicle heritage
gentle comparisons and big smiles
I mimed her
mommy hair was the same

Promoting the thick lush
healthy heavy
of her natural crown
she
wide-eyed and direct
Proclaims
She just wants it to be pretty

A quick scan of the room
trying to find a life raft
Rapunzel
Cinderella
Little Mermaid
all left me limp
looking for ancestral examples
only to come up
permanently weakened
held by laced fronts
and lost edges
how in the afro-sheen
did we get here
like
fresh perm on new growth
I had nothing to grip
missed opportunities
trying to pull visuals
from blinded concepts
I
clearly failed the test

#

Barbershops

Every Saturday he heads
to the barbershop
emotions
are the loudest expressions
boys
are taught to silence

Expectations of manhood
swaddle his infancy
he supposed to man up
shut up
nothing supposed to make him hurt

Skinned knees
on hot summer playgrounds
worn as warrior wounds
proof
he ain't pussy
but don't mind getting some
even if he ain't even seen one

Innocence
and adolescence
stolen by alpha expectations
don't be weak
I need you strong for
the world
and me
we
can't both be scared of the dark
Law 314
don't let them see you cry

you bet not cry
boys don't cry
do they
it didn't hurt that bad
are you bleeding
#butdidyoudie

Stop acting like a girl
Boys don't hit girls
even if they hit you first
be the cowboy you were raised to be
now princess on white horse for me
strong and silent type
I just want you to talk to me
take care of home
fight
stay on defense
ready to attack
and watch this chick flick with me

It can't be that hard to
tell me what you're thinking
open up
visceral reactions
demands
just open up

He
generations iceberg
don't know how to break through
emotions cause upsets
seeking peace in sessions of

barbershop therapy
bound in fragile fabric
he feels most secure
here

Oppression recognizes oppressed
decompression starts at the click
of shaving shears
with razor
inches from his neck
camaraderie
this be a
sanctuary
to refugees
ignoring its still
temporary
from cut to shave
not enough time to
let go it all go
but with a little off the top
it's just enough to
maintain facade

FOODTHATMALNOURISHES

verb/adjective

1. Consuming just to feel full; unable to use it once you've consumed it

2. Taking what is giving instead of what you need to grow

a) settling
b) lacking sustainability

Mothers Prey Pray

Five months along
I prayed for my son
universe
make it easy on me
figured
all I'd have to do was
get him through high school
(No gang affiliation)

Not much to up keep
5 pairs of jeans
multiple shirts
to add variety
ball-fade
or
just a line up
when money was tight
basics
far less stress
than added estrogen

Contemplated and calculated
the involvement of girls
fast-tail
smart mouth
step ahead or two of my son
kind of issues
felt lucky
if a baby was made
it wouldn't live in my house

Try to keep him focused
college

entrepreneur
blue collar
just as long as
he never thought
he could act grown
on leased air
in my house

Worried only about
my suffering
didn't see his journey
failed preparing to prepare him
his position
cast expendable
never the lead
just leading cause of every negative

Just to make it
he'd have to be
aware of his surroundings
even on home turf
no hooded sweaters
jeans
fit to size
with a belt
nothing to stand out
but be different
he'll always fit the description

Colors of the rainbow
he can only choose a handful
Red
Blue
Purple
Yellow
Orange
all off the table

No playing on this block
No cops
You
are what they're protecting most from
No sudden moves
at traffic stops
you don't get warning signs
or warning shots

Mourning
has become
a fixed segment
on my morning news

23 years later
I still pray for my son
universe
kevlar his journey
it will never be
easy on him
guide him through
these blocks
around crooked cops
and home safely

Arrested

Everything was our kind of normal.
Kids running around at 4 AM.
6 kids required an early start.
Jay was sick that morning.
I knew it was going to hit her hard because of all
the mucus.
She threw up on me.
A second shower made me a little late.
This forced me to bag lunches while making
breakfast.
Suddenly, silence.
He walked in with this look.
Lip trembling, and tears in his eyes.
They walked in behind him.
Two plain clothes officers.
I don't remember hearing the doorbell.
I don't remember words or introductions.
Just instructions.
Get your wallet, we need ID.
"Leave your cell phone and any other electronic
devices."
He asked what or maybe where my shoes were.
I think she said,
sandals or something without shoestrings.
No bra if it has wire in it.
My feet went numb.
Started losing feeling in different parts of my body.
The lady cop put the cuffs on.
No bra or panties on, she said I get some issued
once I was housed.
I've never been so aware of my heartbeat before.
4:30 in the morning, freezing cold.

Sweat ran down my armpits soaking the bottom on
my shirt.
I was combusting and freezing at the same time.
I held in my tears just long enough for them to
close the car door.
Didn't realize until that morning,
we lived 15 minutes away from the police station.
Plexiglas so close to my face I could see my
exhale.
Everything about the process, of being processed,
is meant to be dehumanizing.
My knees, against the jagged metal barrier.
Protecting their seats from me
being rubbed raw with every pothole we drove
over.
Not even enough room to sit facing forward.
I spent the entire ride staring at the barrel of a shot
gun.
With every movement, I could hear my shoulder
clicking in and out of place.
Body tense.
I never considered how uncomfortable it would be,
to sit with your hands cuffed behind your back.
Every time I moved, the cuffs tightened around my
wrist.
I couldn't hold back the tears anymore.
Snot was running down my lip.
I gave in to letting it.
Couldn't wipe my face.
I couldn't breathe.
Or maybe I didn't want to anymore
There wasn't enough air in that backseat.

She told me,
"Stop crying, this isn't the hardest part."
I can't believe, I was really going to jail.
I was really, being arrested.
I was having my freedom taken.
Mugshots, health screening, and a blood sample,
to be filed in a database.
Like I was a criminal,
I mean I didn't kill anybody!
The taste of powdered latex lingered after the DNA
swab.
I wish they would have let me explain.
I would have made them understand.
I needed a job.
My babies were hungry.
I'm not a bad person.
Hurried into an old bus hanger.
Muddied, cement floors.
10 other arrested women.
All were instructed to take our clothes off.
Putting on gloves and pulling out flash lights,
they watched us.
Some smiling, and chatting, others looking
annoyed.
Me still crying.
Now standing there exposed.
I felt so naked.
Backs turned, tears falling, trying not to make my
fears known.
I missed the first set of instructions.
The girl next to me whispered, "you're going to
have to bend over."
Bend over?
Bend over?
She shouted "Bend over, spread 'em and cough."

For inspection.
Spread for inspection?
I heard words that I knew but couldn't understand.
Bending over while crying my lungs couldn't
expand enough to cough.
That's when the screaming started.
But I didn't know it was at me.
She raddled off numbers.
Inmate 27385 cough!
The girl next to me tried explaining she just had a
baby.
No one cared.
She stood there, leaking milk from her breast.
I could see the blood running down her leg dripping
on the floor.
No one cared.
We were issued uniforms, shirts too small pants
too big.
Panties too tight.
I didn't get a bra.
All purposed.
Cattle.
Property.
Eyes to the floor.
Shoulder to the wall.
Never make eye contact.
Eye contact with a guard.
You're causing problems.
I couldn't remember my number.
Herded into a single person cell with 30 other
people.
Everything was too close.
I overheard a conversation about how we are lucky.
We made it before the shift changed, which means
we'll get to eat today.

They soon served, what was legally considered a meal.
Some inmates helped to pass out the food.
She walked up to the cell with the blue milk crate, like the ones I remember from elementary school.
Dumping the sandwiches and juice on the floor.
Everybody scrambled.
Pushed and fought.
Like animals.
Snatching food out of each other's hands.
Trading and arguing if someone had more.
Flimsy plastic bags holding half molded peanut butter and jelly.
The juice was outdated by at least a year!
They said at least some of the bread was good.
Pick around it and eat what you can.
Everyone seemed to know the tricks.
Hiding extra jelly packets, to be used later in the stay.
Excited they'd have sweetener for tomorrow's breakfast.
A girl I met on the way to check in looked at me and smiled.
"Don't worry honey, the food is better once you get permanent housing."
I guess I was supposed to be encouraged.

Dearest Mommy

Today
I don't feel like
much of a mother

Disappointment looking back at me
bright eyes
uncut teeth

Still missing 6 hours
out of the 8 of sleep
they say
I'm supposed to get

Dismissing ouches
handing over unopened
generic band aides
with lazy
half assed air kisses
no energy for the
"only mommy can do it"
type pain relief

I don't feel like much of a nurturer
today
balance don't live here

Judgment
broken expectations
tears
man ups
under heated breath
butter breakfast toast today

Words sounding like
How hard is it to find your shoes
carried on
I AIN'T GOT TIME FOR THIS!!!
energy
they feel it
every unspoken intention
self-preservation won't allow me to idle

Idealistically
I'd stop time at 7:39
on a 7:40 deadline
love on them
make a full breakfast
homemade oatmeal
pancakes with
boiled eggs
just the way they like it

I just can't
today

Last few days
my first meal has been dinner
which consisted of scrapes
from their plates
over a full sink
one glove on
washing dishes
planning tomorrow's
gots to's

Football practice
basketball practice
science projects
snacks
I forgot classroom snacks
I didn't even sign up for that

they can be so
inconsiderate
trapped by revolving guilt
they didn't ask to be here
neither did I

Chapped lips
dirty hair
can't remember
if I put on deodorant
attempts to SOS my stress levels
only to get back
Bible thumps and Iyanla quotes
from friends and family
#missmewithallthat

Planting mustard seed
in depleted soil
is a waste
to the sower and reaper
I go without
so they don't have to

I choose last
so they'd always feel ahead

Today
I feel forgotten back here

Today
I don't feel like much of a mother
so you can keep your
empty words of encouragement
pulling up bootstraps
will never work for me
on most days I'm wearing
flip flops
anyway

M.A.G.A My Ass

Politicians, poeting policy.
Passing it off as proficiency.

Suggestio falsi

Perfection
will never be attained
because eyes can't see themselves

We all found out Santa was a fraud
lost teeth have no real value
trying to keep them
will break the bank

Little girls will soon realize
they are not the prettiest things
in the world

Boys
become men
who've fallen from imaginary leaps from
tall buildings
after mommy's good towels
could no longer help him fly

It's the little lies
that lay beneath
the fragile egos
of life's realities
saddest thing is
it doesn't end with adolescents

Men
buy in to the acting on porn

women
really believe princess charming's
coming to save her

and all she needs
is the right shoes

Bullshit on the news
like
Africans in Liberia
have no chance against Ebola
viruses
just appear
and test subjects
are a part of the cure

That plane
just so happened
to have gone missing
now houses 239 missing
all in the name of religion

The black community,
it will be saved by its next leader
and liters of water
won't soon be coveted like gold
where displays of wealth
can only be bought with the currency
of lost souls
worn down soles
from peaceful protest
and marches
will soon make a difference

More Lies

There is equality
in equilibrium
in laymen terms
we can agree to disagree

that the lives of
black and brown boys
are valued
that
a mother's tears
will ever dry bitter sweet
instead of salty
and at any point
it's ok
for the government
to profit from slavery
no matter what they call it
#thenewjimcrow

Skin bleaching
started on pyramid walls
they tried to erase our majesty
from their stories
just because they can't duplicate it
aliens made it

Overcrowded classrooms
teach-less teachers
book-less lessons
still being defined as education
and we pay for it
for-profit higher education
are the real loans of predators
3rd grade test scores
used in prison data collection
but
they say there's no systematics
in the plan
These crows
are still protecting Jim's land

the just as fat and full
eating crumbs
right from Rockefeller's hands

*Suggestio falsi: law: suggestion of an untruth: false
statement as opposed to suppression of the truth*

Wild Peaches

Wild peaches grow in Mississippi
locals won't eat
because
of what they're fertilized with

Trees whose leaves
pass down stories
of involuntary manslaughter
its roots
guilty by association

Everyone seems oblivious
another boy shot dead today
mothers are burying their sons
we still don't know
what to call them

There will be a local story
excuses of badged privileges
turn national news because
#BlueLivesMattertoo

Reckless rhetoric
mistaken for a movement
we shouldn't have to tell them
our lives matter

There's a marked season
we should be used to it by now
for licensed hunters
improper kill methods
fines and jail time

This shooting
these two shootings
the boy who had the candy
who let the other boy
hold his toy gun
who told the other boy
he'd be ok
walking to the store
they know the man
on the corner
selling cigarettes
on the day the cops
gave that man a ride

Will all be over shadowed
by breaking news
coverage
inhumane treatment
of a dolphin
everyone's cameras
were working
no lost footage
no indictment
he feared for his life

There will be outrage
internal disruptions
post
shares
comments
live feeds leading to
lifeless ideas

The law says
it's illegal
to leave your kill

in the streets
but not on the trees
strange fruit
runs through these roots
eulogies whispered among the leaves
revenge lives in its shade

No more tag lines
there's blood at our feet
passed down
in their privilege
lineage at risk of extinction

For licensed hunters
the law says
changes in predatory
prey ratios
the prey
must be protected
or it will become
an endangered species
maybe black people
should consult with PETA
they have laws
to protect them

Recidivism

Once added in
forever
a subtracted total
of sum
redemption don't live here

Paid debts to a society
that will never
honor your receipts
more than
scarlet letter
condemnation
spoken from the lips
of everyone you'll meet
Even
before you've met

Judged
convicted
by so called peers
now
legally required
to surrender all your secrets
on dotted lines
checking boxes
on applications
that box you in
on extra sheets of paper
trying to human explanations
failure to do so
proves you are
what they say

Counting on fuck ups
increases the stock rates
no one has vacancies
in their vacancies
after your background is checked

Permitted bodies
restricted minds
monthly meetings with desks
nothing but shuffled papers
scuffled through a system
twisted broken

Perfectly crafted cracks
for you to fall
stubbed toe
on diabetic foot
potential amputee
handicapped
for the rest of your life

Convicted
marginalized
you become description
instead of human
thought all mistake
no lesson learned
can't vote
no job
life insurance
denied
how is life lived

when
second chances are
above your means
worthless dead or alive

Said the Collector to the Debtor

* Response to Paul Lawrence Dunbar's The Debt

Make good on the loan I gave
Now you owe, failing to read the small print, made
you my slave
Every week, between paychecks, struggle and
stress
Don't think about defaulting, we have you and yo
mamas address
Payday loans, to pay back payday loans, this vicious
cycle your only option
Racking up more debt, to pay back debate is now
your indemnification
Funny how your wants easily outweighed
responsibilities
Now you're crying, trying to make payment
arrangements on your utilities
It was written, listed for you to see
Not our fault you missed the hidden fee

I named her Ciera Rose

Devonte Hart's biological mother, Sherry Davis:
"They gave my kids to monsters." This was the
opening line of an article I read, on oregonlive.com.
The story about the 6 black children killed by their
adopted parents. The autopsy reports show; the
adults were drunk. The children had Benadryl in
their system. I was hit with a swell of emotions all
at once. The fact that, these children, senselessly
lost their lives. The fact that they were supposed
to be taken from an unhealthy situation, and ended
up murdered, was infuriating. There was evidence
of abuse, starvation, and causing bodily harm.
Their foster mother was found guilty of assault,
and never spent a day in jail. Paraded them around
the neighbored, to show their black children were
obedient. I'm pissed! I'm disgusted with the
system. But I also feel guilty. These are our babies.
This is our village. They are counting on us to save
them. Before her last interview, Sherry started her
statement with correction. "Before I say anything,
you all have been spelling my baby's name wrong.
I named her Ciera Rose."

His birth mother said
I could tell my baby
had something to say
I could tell
he was too scared to speak
giving out hugs
should have been a happy thing

Front cover of every newspaper
all over social media feeds

locked arms around blue walls
wet face
brown skinned boy

We saw you
stood out of
freeze frame
odd
like
which one of these things
don't belong

They saw you
covered eyes
and muffled ears
your face
encyclopedia britannica
there was more
to your cover
in those final moments
figuring out
which left is right

Clever distractions
we don't hear no stories
about the hearts of
brown skinned boys
unless they're condolences
unless they're
mysteriously missing
from found bodies

Trying to piece together thoughts
feeling everything

and numbing
they never headline your gentle
they don't offer you empathy
they plaster brown boy faces
across newspapers
aggressive
new age lynching

Mandated reporters
dismissed distress
seeping from your bruised skin
from your sister's
bloody finger tips
swollen knees
she jumped from her bedroom window
hoping to find food

Slave like repercussions
you all wore welts of desperation
Domestic assault charges
thrown out
sentence to 90 days
didn't even serve them
they say
black folks have thicker skin
they don't feel the same pain

You are not the first
you haven't been the only
we cannot allow any others
no more silence
DNA carries memories
ancestral wombs weeps
for your absent
forgive us
we failed to village
your spirits

Regarding Pink Beanies

*When there isn't enough religion, or justice in the
courtrooms, manhood in the nation. If it should
require lynching to protect a women's position and
delicacies from raving human beast. I say lynching
a thousand times a week is necessary. I would
rather see a thousand die before a Negro goes to
the polls before a white woman.*
  *- Rebecca Latimer Felton (Founding member
   of the Feminist/Suffrage Movement)*

Your pink kitty beanie
doesn't match my RBG
We ain't neva
wore the same weary

You mad
I won't force wear
on the soles of my shoes
for your tiled roads
it's clear
your privilege
is showing
you expect me
to brace body
against your picket fences

Not today
I won't be marching
in protest
of your perceived
mistreatment
nor breaking glass ceiling
in your glass house

we
ain't neva been
sisters in suffrage
we
nursed your babies
washed your floors
served your meals
and your men
at Seneca Falls

Stood
in the back of your lines
during marches
your wins
have never
increased our stats
or
bettered our communities
equal
not even on the table
separate
always on order

You pushed naming rights
equal pay
strengthening
your position
in supremacy
we fight to be treated
as human
to be educated
for the lives
of our children
our men

Our resistance
is in our existence
you've turned blind eye

to the poisoning of our children
wombs
and water
not allowed to whistle
walk on sidewalks
drink water when thirsty

Where were your pastel prints
during forced sterilization
or in the aftermath of Tuskegee
we are still birthing affected babies
our wombs don't grieve the same

We weren't accepted in the N.O.W*
back then
we ain't neva
shared the same pain
*Alice Walker said "Womanism is to feminism, as
purple is to lavender."*
you
not seeing color
won't ever clear the picture

Besides
your pink kitty hat
gets lint in my locs
me and my folks
fight together
our struggles
never gender specific
we need each other
we're on the front lines
I'm reminded everyday
I am
a
Black Woman

N.O.W.: National Organization for Women

Acknowledgments

Putting this project together was harder than I thought and more freeing than I could have ever imagined. I wouldn't have been able to do it without the help of my village. My gratitude to the many people who saw me through the insecurities of my words, provided support, read through the many preceding drafts. Those who assisted in the editing, proofreading, and design. To the creators of every open mic I've had a chance to perform, and those in my future. Lastly, to everyone who has ever shared a kind word, encouraging hug, silent prayer, or a meal (especially if you paid).

You are appreciated!

#webefamily

About the Author

Alexandra O. Photography

October B.L.U
(Breathing Life
into the Universe)
is an emerging
spoken word artist;
born and raised in
South Central, Los
Angeles. She has a
Bachelors of Science
in Psychology, and
has been writing
for over 19 years.
It wasn't until attending various workshops,
developing her confidence, that October B.L.U
started taking to the stage. Since 2011, she has
been a featured poet at numerous events including,
KPCC In Person Unheard LA, and the Los Angeles
Pan African Film Festival. She is also a contributor
to many poetry anthologies including Voices from
Leimert Park Redux and Sounds of the Waters.